Wall Paintings

Nathaniel Harris

WAYLAND

First published in 2008 by Wayland

Copyright © Wayland 2008

Wayland
338 Euston Road
London NW1 3BH

Wayland
Level 17/207 Kent Street
Sydney NSW 2000

The right of Nathaniel Harris to be identified as the author of the work has been asserted by him in accordance with the Copyright, Designs and Patents Act 1988.

A catalogue record for this book is available from the British Library.

ISBN 978 0 7502 5066 5

Senior Editor: Claire Shanahan
Designer: Rachel Hamdi/Holly Fulbrook
Project Maker: Anna-Marie d'Cruz
Models: Shannon O' Leary, Ross Zavros
Photographer: Andy Crawford

Printed in China

Wayland is a division of Hachette Children's Books,
an Hachette Livre UK company.

Contents

What are wall paintings?

Wall paintings are pictures that have been painted directly on to the surfaces of walls. They are different from pictures simply hung on walls, which can be moved at any time. Wall paintings become a permanent part of a house or site. They are also known as **murals**, from the Latin word for 'wall'.

The earliest surviving paintings were done about 34,000 years ago, on the walls of caves and on rocks used as shelters by wandering groups of people. The earliest paintings of all were probably hand stencils, made by placing a hand against a rock and blowing or flinging powdered colour at it. When the hand was removed, its shape could still be seen inside the surrounding colour (see the illustration below). Stone Age artists in Europe went on to produce superbly lifelike animal paintings, working deep in caves. Some peoples, such as Australia's **Aborigines**, have continued to make rock paintings until very recent times (page 18). When people began to build houses, palaces and places of worship, they decorated many walls and ceilings with painted images. For centuries, such murals were the most important type of picture.

◀ *Stencilled hands and other paintings cover the walls of the Cave of the Hands in the province of Santa Cruz, Argentina. Some of these images are 9,000 years old. Many rock paintings discovered in Europe are even older, dating from as much as 25,000 years earlier.*

Great wall paintings were created by the ancient Egyptians (see page 10), the Greeks and Romans (see right), the Maya of Central America, and the great civilizations of Asia (see page 9).

A strong Christian tradition of murals developed in Europe, and especially Italy. There, artists such as Giotto (see page 12), Michelangelo and Raphael (see page 8) pioneered a great new movement, the Renaissance. Later, murals made a powerful impact in the hands of modern masters such as Diego Rivera (see page 14).

Not all murals are the work of professional artists. People sometimes paint the outsides of their houses for traditional or political reasons (see page 20). And there are also paintings done on public surfaces without permission, known as graffiti. Usually spray-painted, these range from scribbles to skilful works of art.

▲ Lost in thought, a girl wonders what she should write. This Roman mural dates from the 1st century CE. Originally in Pompeii, it is now in the National Museum, Naples, Italy.

How to use this book

Background information on each wall painting featured, including its creator, date, location and history

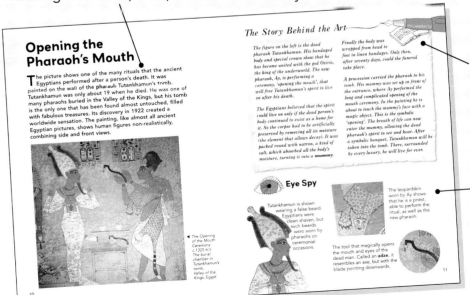

This section tells you about the story behind each wall painting

Take a closer look at the details in each wall painting

How are wall paintings made?

Until modern times, all the colours used in painting were made from natural sources, such as minerals and plants. These paint colours are called **pigments**. Usually pigments are ground into a powder and then mixed with a substance to make them fluid. Such a substance is called a **medium**. Egg, oil and wax are among the mediums used in making paint. Prehistoric painters are believed to have used water or animal fat as a medium. They used shells for holding their colours, and probably made their brushes from animal hair tied to sticks.

▲ The School of Athens is an imaginary group portrait of ancient Greek philosophers. It was painted in 1511 by the Italian Renaissance artist Raphael, and is now in the Vatican Museum, Rome.

The most common mural technique has involved spreading a layer of plaster on the wall before painting. This is done to create a surface that will be smooth and will also absorb the paint. **Medieval** Italian artists like Giotto developed an effective technique which they called *fresco* ('fresh'). They used water-based colours to paint on newly made plaster while it was still slightly damp. As the plaster and paint dried, chemical changes fused them into a single substance, so that the paint was no longer likely to fall away from its plaster base.

► *This beautiful 17th-century Persian painting shows King Abbas II being served by a courtier. It belongs to a group of murals in a pleasure pavilion, the Palace of Forty Pillars, built for the Persian kings at Isfahan in Iran.*

Artists who painted frescoes had to work quickly. A new section of wet plaster was laid on the wall each working day, and all of it had to be painted before the plaster dried out. Artists developed methods of rapidly transferring outline drawings on to the plaster. For large-scale projects, scaffolding had to be put up so that the artist could reach every part of the surface. Most artists employed teams of assistants. As well as working quickly, the artist often had to create a picture that could be seen and understood from a distance or from below. For both of these reasons, most frescoes are bold and colourful paintings in which detail is less important than impact.

Many Italian frescoes are still in good condition, but those in the damper atmosphere of northern countries tended to decay. This was one reason for the development of oil painting – painting done on canvas, using oil instead of water as a medium. Oil paintings may be large or small. Many were and are intended to hang on a wall. But in recent times, oil paintings on very large canvases have also been made as murals, permanently attached to the wall or ceiling.

Design a graffiti poster

What you do:

1 Take a look at the kind of writing, symbols, **tags** and illustrations used in graffiti in your local area. You can also use the Internet for research and study different designs of the printed letters used in magazines and newspapers.

You will need:
A4 paper
• coloured pencils, chalks, pastels and felt-tip pens • large sheets of sugar paper • different coloured marker pens
• selection of newspapers, magazines and graffiti type
• double-sided sticky tape or drawing pins

Jack   Snowy/rabbit
Blue   Birds
Television   Animals
Music   Sport
Books   Friends
Cat/Fidget

2 Brainstorm on paper. Think of all the different words that you could graffiti – consider what subjects you like in school, what you like to do in your spare time, what kind of food you like to eat, what makes you happy or sad, and so on. If you're working with a friend or classmate, why not discuss each other's lists to give you ideas?

3 Using your research, experiment with different styles of lettering and various materials to write on the A4 paper. Try to incorporate an illustration or tag with the word so that they work together. For example, you could fill the spaces between letters and add graffiti 'accessories' such as crowns, arrows, haloes or shadows to the letters. Your graffiti statement should be easily readable, but it's important to have fun with it and play with the words and tags.

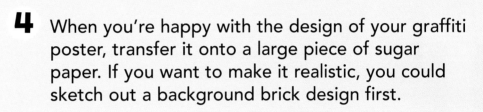

4 When you're happy with the design of your graffiti poster, transfer it onto a large piece of sugar paper. If you want to make it realistic, you could sketch out a background brick design first.

5 Fix the sugar paper on to a wall, using double-sided sticky tape or drawing pins. If you are working with friends or classmates, ask an adult if you can use a whole wall to place your graffiti posters together.

You could make the graffiti poster part of a graffiti mood wall, an area dedicated to you and your favourite things rather than just one statement piece.

Create a mural

This is a large-scale mural based on a famous work of art that you can make with friends or classmates.

What you do:

1 Print out from the Internet a colour copy of a famous work of art or use a colour photocopy from a book.

When choosing which artwork to use, think about the materials and technique used by the original artist, as you will need to imitate these for a true result. For instance, Van Gogh used large paintstrokes in his *Starry Night* painting.

2 Draw horizontal and vertical lines to create a grid of nine squares on the work of art. If you're working with friends or classmates, you will take a square each to work on.

Top Tip!
Use a fine pen or pencil when making your grid so the lines don't cover much of the artwork.

3 Once you have decided which square of the grid you are going to re-create, study the square carefully. Consider the size and positioning of the different details in the square and how they relate to one another.

Top Tip!
Use a magnifying glass if you want to have a close look at the square.

4 Lightly sketch the outline in pencil on an A3 page. Try to re-create the size and positioning of each detail in your square to fill the page.

5 Once you're happy with your outline, start painting, again copying the colours and shading in the square.

6 When you and your friends have all the finished squares, put them together and the edges should match up to make one big picture.

Make a fresco

What you do:

1 Cut the burlap into roughly A4 size. Place the burlap on top of a piece of corrugated or strong cardboard to protect the table from wet plaster and to allow you to move it easily later on.

2 Mix the Plaster of Paris according to the instructions on the packet.

3 Pour the Plaster of Paris in the centre of the burlap square. Using a spoon, spread it out in a thin layer from the middle into a rectangular shape, so that no burlap is visible underneath the plaster. Leave about 1cm of burlap around the edge. Allow the plaster to dry for an hour or more.

4 While the plaster is drying, plan and design your sketch on paper.

Top Tip!
Gently shake the sides of the cardboard to get rid of any air bubbles in the Plaster of Paris.

26

5 Use sandpaper to gently smooth out any bumps or sharp edges in the plaster.

6 Lightly dampen the plaster with a wet sponge. This will help the watercolour paints to soak into the plaster.

7 With watercolour paints, draw and colour in your design on the re-dampened plaster.

8 Once you have finished colouring and the plaster is dry, make the fresco look like a centuries-old work by bending it in your hands to create chips and breaks in it. Don't worry about the plaster falling off the burlap – it will have stuck to it when drying.

9 Seal the plaster with a thin layer of PVA glue, allowing it to seep in to the cracks.

Glossary

Aborigines the people who inhabited Australia before Europeans arrived. The adjective is Aboriginal

adze tool like an axe, but with a blade pointing downwards, at right angles to the shaft

Aztecs the people who dominated most of Mexico from about 1450 CE until the Spanish arrived in 1519 CE

disciples followers of a religious teacher

Easter Rising 1916 Irish Rebellion against British rule

figurehead the carved human or other figure frequently placed on the prow (front) of a ship

fresco Italian word meaning 'fresh'. It describes the technique of painting on fresh, still damp plaster

halo an artistic symbol in the form of a circle of light or a golden disc, above or around the head of a holy or divine person

incendiary bomb a bomb designed to start a fire once it hits its target

medieval describes anything to do with the Middle Ages (about 500-1500 CE)

medium oil, water or any other substance used to make pigment (see below) into paint

mummy a dead body, preserved by the removal of all its moisture. This has been done by humans, but sometimes also occurs naturally

mural a wall painting

Neptune Roman sea god

pharaoh a king of ancient Egypt

pigments the colours used in painting in their dry form, before they are mixed with a medium (see above)

Quinkans in Australian Aboriginal belief, frightening spirits of the dead

stingray a flat fish with a barbed, poisonous tail

tags used in graffiti to describe a person's chosen nickname or personally designed signature

tribute money or goods paid to a dominant power or individual

trompe l'oeil a French term meaning 'deceive the eye'. It describes paintings so lifelike that viewers may believe they are looking at real creatures or objects

zombies imaginary humans without minds or souls, found in many myths and stories

Find out more

Books to read

Aboriginal Art of Australia by Carol Finlay (Lerner, 1995)
Diego Rivera by Joanne Mattern (Checkerboard, 2005)
Giotto and Medieval Art by Lucia Corrain (Macdonald, 1995)
The Life and Work of Michelangelo Buonarroti by Richard Tames (Heinemann, 2007)
Painting Murals: Images, Ideas, Techniques by Patricia Seligman (Macdonald, 1987)
Prehistoric Art by Susie Hodge (Heinemann.2006)
Stencils and Screens by Susie O'Reilly (Wayland, 1993)
The Usborne Book of Stencil Fun by Ray Gibson (Usborne Publishing, 1995)
Trompe L'Oeil by Roberta Gordon-Smith (David & Charles, 1997)
What Makes a Raphael a Raphael? By Richard Mühlberger (Cherrytree, 1994)

Websites to visit

BBC Northern Ireland Learning (www.bbc.co.uk/northernireland/schools/4_11/primaryart/) has three detailed class projects for colourful murals based on the natural world.

Thinkquest.org (www.library.thinkquest.org/CR0210200/ancient_rome/art.htm) is a site with good illustrations and interesting information about Roman art. The section about creating Roman artefacts tells you how to make a simple fresco with Plaster of Paris and watercolours.

Places to go

The British Museum, the Victoria and Albert Museum and the London Museum, all in London, have good collections; the British Museum's Egyptian wall paintings are outstanding. The Banqueting House in Whitehall, London, has a ceiling painted by the famous 17th century artist Peter Paul Rubens.

England's country houses are filled with murals, for example Louis Laguerre's works at Chatsworth, Derbyshire, and Blenheim Palace, Oxfordshire.

There are interesting wall paintings in many other places. Examples are Birmingham's Piccadilly Arcade (the ceiling), Manchester Town Hall, Sandham Memorial Chapel in Burghclere, Hampshire, and Edinburgh's National Portrait Gallery. Very recent murals on city sites include the Cable Street Mural at Shadwell, east London, and the Stockwell Memorial Gardens Mural in south London.

Index

Photos or pictures are shown below in bold, **like this**.